Crafts in a Snap!

FAR OUT FLOWERS

by Jane Yates

BEARPORT
PUBLISHING

Minneapolis, Minnesota

CREATE!

Credits:
5 top right, Alexandr Makarov/Shutterstock.com; 5 upper middle, © Crackerclips|Dreamstime.com; 5 upper bottom, Lyudmila Suvorova/Shutterstock.com; 11 bottom left, iofoto/Shutterstock.com; 22 left © fightbegin; 22 right © LACROIX CHRISTINE; all other photos © Austen Photography

Bearport Publishing Company Product Development Team
President: Jen Jenson; Director of Product Development: Spencer Brinker; Senior Editor: Allison Juda; Editor: Charly Haley; Associate Editor: Naomi Reich; Senior Designer: Colin O'Dea; Associate Designer: Elena Klinkner; Associate Designer: Kayla Eggert; Product Development Assistant: Anita Stasson

Produced for Bearport Publishing by BlueAppleWorks Inc.
Managing Editor for BlueAppleWorks: Melissa McClellan
Art Director: T.J. Choleva

Library of Congress Cataloging-in-Publication Data

Names: Yates, Jane, author.
Title: Far out flowers / by Jane Yates.
Description: Minneapolis, Minnesota : Bearport Publishing, [2023] | Series: Create! | Includes bibliographical references and index.
Identifiers: LCCN 2022033385 (print) | LCCN 2022033386 (ebook) | ISBN 9798885094399 (library binding) | ISBN 9798885096768 (ebook)
Subjects: LCSH: Artificial flowers--Juvenile literature. | Flowers in art--Juvenile literature. | Refuse as art materia--Juvenile literature. | Trash art--Juvenile literature.
Classification: LCC TT890 .Y29 2023 (print) | LCC TT890 (ebook) | DDC 745.92--dc23/eng/20220819
LC record available at https://lccn.loc.gov/2022033385
LC ebook record available at https://lccn.loc.gov/2022033386

For more information, write to Bearport Publishing, 5357 Penn Avenue South, Minneapolis, MN 55419.

Contents

Far Out Flowers
in a Snap!

Ready for some fun? Let's do some quick art projects and make flowers from **reusable** materials. This helps reduce trash and keeps waste out of recycling or trash bins. Before we get started, take a look at these tips to help you make super crafts in a snap:

- Read all instructions first. Ask an adult for help if you have any questions.

- Cover your work area with newspaper to protect the surface.

- Gather your materials and tools before you start.

- Get creative when looking for materials. You can use cardboard from cereal boxes or other packaging. Ask friends and family for old scraps of clothing, yarn, or other items.

- When gluing things together, gently press the pieces until they stay stuck in place.

- Be careful when using scissors. Always keep your fingers away from the area you are cutting.

- Tissue paper is fun to work with. However, it is **delicate** and tears easily. So, handle it with care.

- After each project, be sure to clean up your work area. Put away all your tools. Save any leftover materials to use for another craft project.

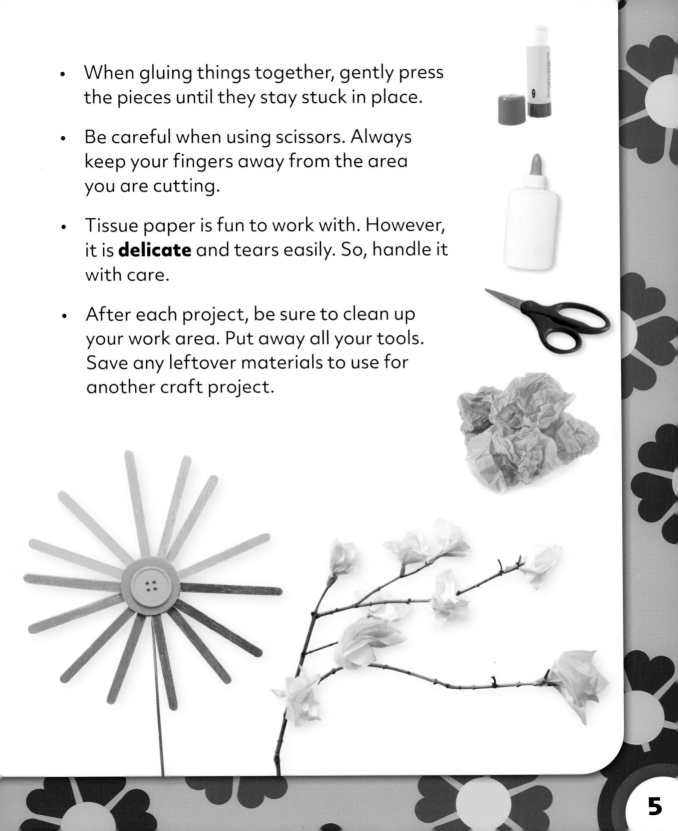

Totally Tulips

Tulips are often some of the first flowers of spring. Their colorful petals are a sign of the changing seasons. Make your own colorful tulips from an egg carton to have a little spring at any time of the year.

You Will Need

- ✓ Scissors
- ✓ An egg carton
- ✓ A pencil
- ✓ Pipe cleaners
- ✓ Buttons
- ✓ Craft paints
- ✓ A paintbrush

1 Use scissors to cut one egg cup out of the egg carton.

2 Then, cut the top of the cup into petal shapes.

3 Turn the cup over, and ask an adult to help you use a pencil to poke two holes into the bottom.

4 Bend a pipe cleaner and slide each end through the openings of a button.

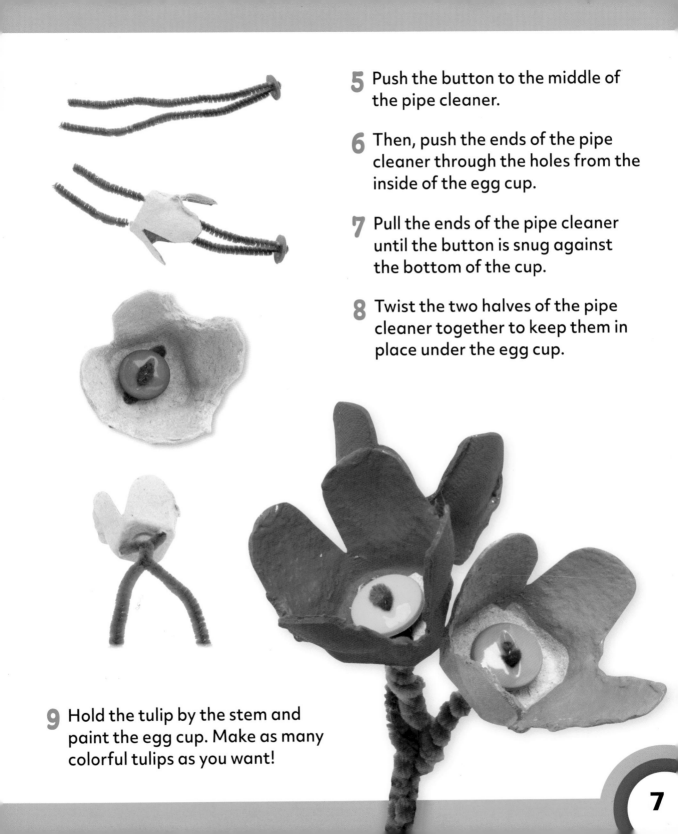

5 Push the button to the middle of the pipe cleaner.

6 Then, push the ends of the pipe cleaner through the holes from the inside of the egg cup.

7 Pull the ends of the pipe cleaner until the button is snug against the bottom of the cup.

8 Twist the two halves of the pipe cleaner together to keep them in place under the egg cup.

9 Hold the tulip by the stem and paint the egg cup. Make as many colorful tulips as you want!

Jumbo Flower

Make a flower as big as your head! First, you'll fold tissue paper into something small. Then, when you unfold it, you'll find a big bloom!

1 Stack all the larger sheets of tissue paper on top of one another.

2 Use scissors to cut **slits** into the long sides of the smaller sheets of tissue paper. These slits should be about 2 in. (5 cm) long with about ½ in. (1.5 cm) between them.

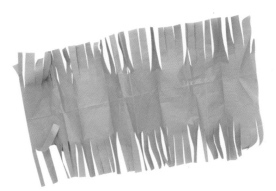

3 Place the cut sheets of tissue paper in the center of the stack of large pieces.

4 Next, **accordion fold** the tissue paper. Start along an edge that has all the layers of paper and fold the bottom of the stack up 2 in. (5 cm). Press down to make a **crease**.

5 Hold onto the folded edge, and carefully flip the papers over. Fold the bottom up 2 in. (5 cm) again and press to make another crease.

6 Continue flipping, folding, and creasing until you get to the end of the paper. This will leave you with a narrow strip.

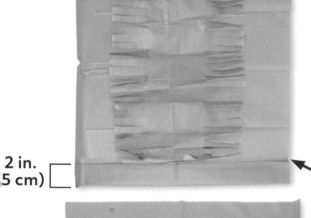

2 in.
5 cm)

Fold here

in.
cm)

Fold here

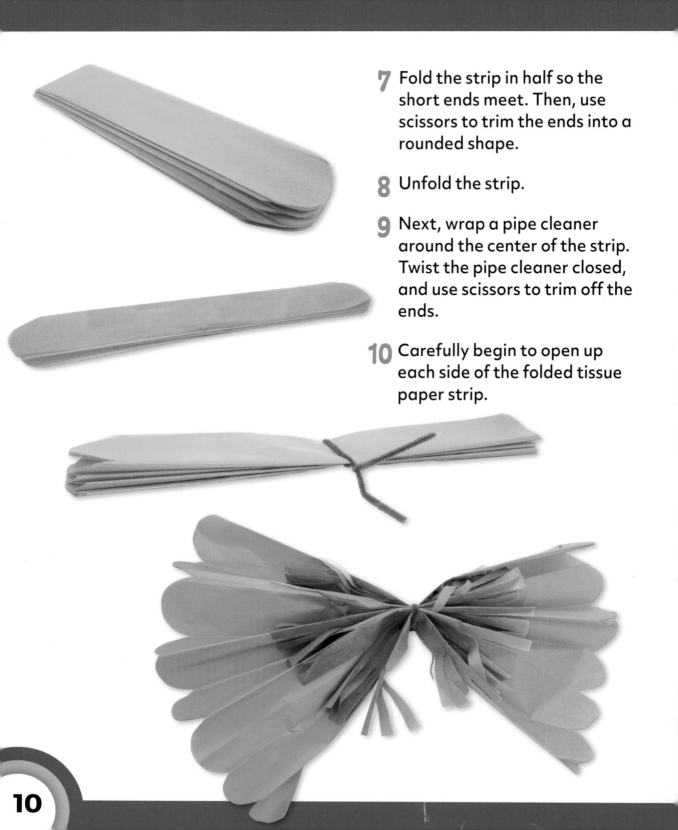

7 Fold the strip in half so the short ends meet. Then, use scissors to trim the ends into a rounded shape.

8 Unfold the strip.

9 Next, wrap a pipe cleaner around the center of the strip. Twist the pipe cleaner closed, and use scissors to trim off the ends.

10 Carefully begin to open up each side of the folded tissue paper strip.

11 Open the flower by gently separating the pieces of paper.

12 Fluff the sheets until you are happy with the shape of your colorful jumbo flower.

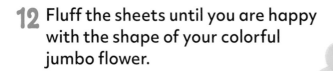

Bloom on a Loom

Make a circle **loom** to weave a wonderful flower. It's amazing what can blossom from some scraps and a little creativity!

You Will Need

- ✔ Scissors
- ✔ The lid from a large yogurt container
- ✔ A marker
- ✔ A ruler
- ✔ Masking tape
- ✔ Thick yarn
- ✔ A craft stick

1 Use scissors to carefully cut off the outer rim of the yogurt lid. Then, use a marker to draw a circle in the center of the lid about 1 in. (2.5 cm) wide.

2 Next, use a marker and a ruler to draw three lines through the center of the circle, dividing the lid into six triangle shapes.

3 Cut along the lines from the edges of the lid to the inner circle. This will make six **slits** in the lid.

4 Tape one end of the yarn to the lid loom.

5 Then, turn the loom over and pull the yarn through one of the slits.

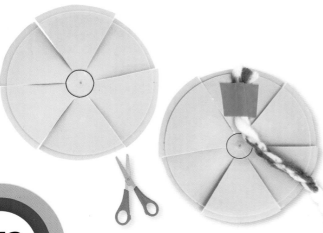

6 Start to weave the yarn over and under the sections of the lid once around. When you get back to the start, three sections will have yarn over them.

7 Next, wrap yarn *over* the section where you stopped and start weaving in the opposite direction. Stop when each section has yarn over it once.

8 When you get back to the start, wrap yarn *under* the section where you stopped. Change direction again and weave once around the circle.

9 Keep weaving once around, changing direction, and then going back around. Each section should end with an even number of rows of yarn.

10 Once the loom is covered, turn it over and tape the end of the yarn to the loom. Trim off any extra yarn. Then, slip a craft stick under the yarn as a stem.

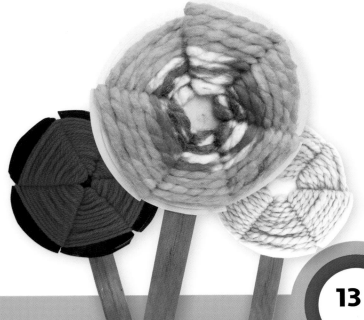

Freaky Flower Faces

Create freaky flower faces by combining animal and human features into a strange blooming sight! This **collage** technique is sure to make a fun **bouquet** of weirdness.

You Will Need

✔ Old magazines or catalogs that show animals and humans
✔ Scissors
✔ Thin cardboard
✔ White school glue
✔ Thick cardboard

1 First, cut out an animal head from an old magazine. Then, find human eyes and a mouth, and cut them out.

2 Cut eight triangles of roughly the same size from the thin cardboard. These will be petals for your flower.

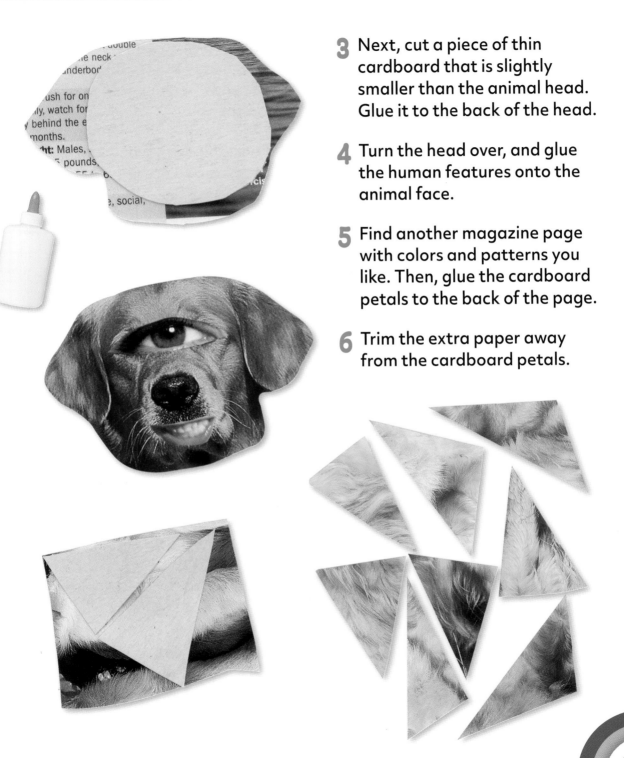

3 Next, cut a piece of thin cardboard that is slightly smaller than the animal head. Glue it to the back of the head.

4 Turn the head over, and glue the human features onto the animal face.

5 Find another magazine page with colors and patterns you like. Then, glue the cardboard petals to the back of the page.

6 Trim the extra paper away from the cardboard petals.

7 Lay the petals out in a flower shape, and put a drop of glue at the end of each petal, near the center point.

8 Place the animal head on top of the glue and press down.

9 For a stem, cut a long strip from thick cardboard. Glue a piece of a magazine page to this strip. Then, trim off any extra paper.

10 Glue the stem to the back of the flower.

11 Make several freaky flowers in different shapes and sizes to create a big, bizarre bouquet!

A Branch of Blossoms

The delicate flowers of cherry blossoms last for only a couple of weeks. But you can enjoy cherry blossoms year-round with this beautiful tissue paper craft.

You Will Need

- ✓ A long, thin branch that has a few small twigs attached
- ✓ Scissors
- ✓ Pink tissue paper
- ✓ A pencil
- ✓ Green masking tape

1 Make your branch into the shape you want by breaking off any extra twigs. If you can't find a real branch for this craft, see what you have that could act as a branch.

2 Then, use scissors to cut pink tissue paper into an even number of 3-in. (7.5-cm) squares. You will need two squares for each blossom.

3 Place one square on top of another so the corners of each square are not lined up.

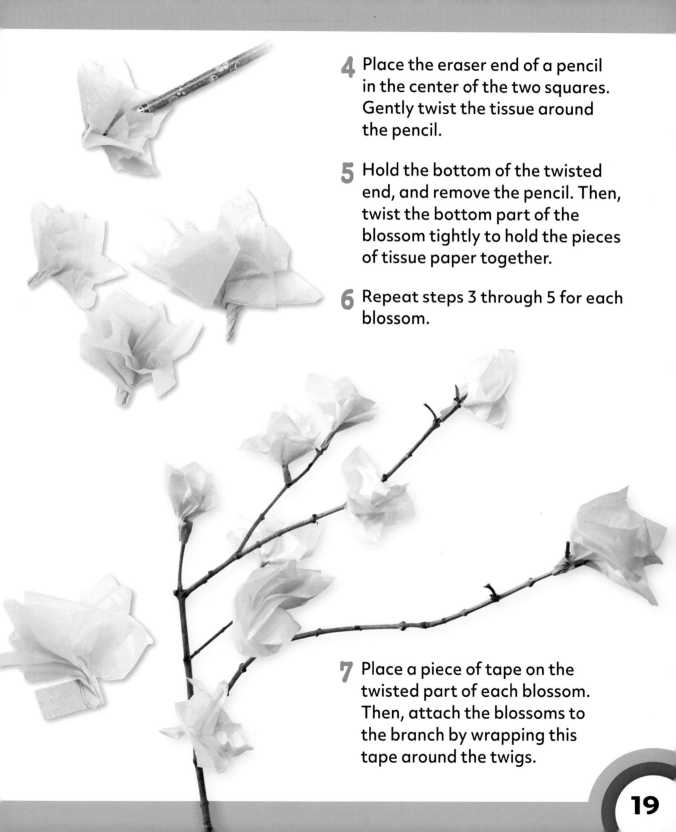

4 Place the eraser end of a pencil in the center of the two squares. Gently twist the tissue around the pencil.

5 Hold the bottom of the twisted end, and remove the pencil. Then, twist the bottom part of the blossom tightly to hold the pieces of tissue paper together.

6 Repeat steps 3 through 5 for each blossom.

7 Place a piece of tape on the twisted part of each blossom. Then, attach the blossoms to the branch by wrapping this tape around the twigs.

Flower Power

Make a daisy with all the colors of a rainbow and bring some flower power to your day.

You Will Need

- ✔ 7 colorful crayons
- ✔ 14 craft sticks
- ✔ Scissors
- ✔ Thick cardboard
- ✔ White school glue
- ✔ Masking tape
- ✔ A wooden skewer
- ✔ A button

1 Use crayons to color one side of each craft stick. Make two sticks in each color of the rainbow.

2 Then, use scissors to cut three circles from thick cardboard, each about 2 in. (5 cm) wide.

3 Cover one circle with glue.

4 Press the ends of seven craft sticks into the glue in rainbow order. Be sure to space them evenly around the circle.

5 Place the second cardboard circle on top and press down to glue the stack together.

6 Next, cover the top cardboard circle with more glue.

7 Press the remaining craft sticks into the glue, keeping each stick next to its matching color.

8 Place the third cardboard circle on top. This is the front of your flower.

9 Turn the flower over, and tape a wooden skewer to the back.

10 Lastly, flip the flower back over and glue a button to the middle of the cardboard circle.

Trash into Treasure!

Every day, Americans create enough waste to fill 63,000 garbage trucks! They toss about 22 billion plastic bottles a year and throw out enough paper to make a 12-foot (3.7-m) tall wall that could stretch from New York City to Los Angeles.

What can we do instead of trashing the planet? Make more art! Artists everywhere are using trash for creative projects. These artists remind us that we have too much garbage by taking on the problem in a beautiful way.

In Toronto, Canada, a colorful archway was made from old pool noodles.

In Alcoutim, Portugal, you can find this cute, colorful cat made from recycled garbage.

Glossary

accordion fold to fold something back and forth into evenly spaced creases that look like the middle part of an accordion musical instrument

bouquet a bunch of flowers

collage a kind of art made of various materials glued on a surface

crease a line made on paper or cloth by folding and pressing

delicate thin or weak

loom a tool for weaving

reusable able to be used again

slits long, narrow cuts

Index

Read More

McLeod, Kimberly. *Cut & Color Crafts for Kids: 35 Super Cool Activities That Bring Recycled Materials to Life.* Salem, MA: Page Street Publishing, 2022.

Rathburn, Betsy. *Egg Carton Crafts (Express! Easy Upcycled Crafts).* Minneapolis: Bellwether Media, 2022.

Schuette, Sarah L. *10-Minute Paper Projects (10-Minute Makers).* North Mankato, MN: Capstone Press, 2020.

Learn More Online

1. Go to **www.factsurfer.com** or scan the QR code below.
2. Enter "**Far Out Flowers**" into the search box.
3. Click on the cover of this book to see a list of websites.

About the Author

Jane Yates has loved crafting all her life and has tried every craft there is. She has written more than 20 craft books.